D1432613

Tom
BRADY
VS.
Joe
MONTANA

BY BARRY WILNER

SportsZone

An Imprint of Abdo Publishing
abdopublishing.com

abdopublishing.com

Published by Abdo Publishing, a division of ABDO, PO Box 398166, Minneapolis, Minnesota 55439. Copyright © 2018 by Abdo Consulting Group, Inc. International copyrights reserved in all countries. No part of this book may be reproduced in any form without written permission from the publisher. SportsZone™ is a trademark and logo of Abdo Publishing.

Printed in the United States of America, North Mankato, Minnesota
102017
012018

Cover Photo: G. Newman Lowrance/AP Images, left; Eric Risberg/AP Images, right
Interior Photos: Daniel Dunn/Icon Sportswire/Newscom, 4–5; John Gaps III/AP Images, 5; NFL Photos/AP Images, 6–7, 26; Matthew Healey/UPI/Newscom, 9; Kevin Dietsch/UPI/ Newscom, 11; Greg Trott/AP Images, 12–13; Tony Tomsic/AP Images, 14; Kevin Hoffman/ USA Today Sports/Newscom, 17; John Iacono/SI/Icon SMI/Newscom, 18–19; Geoff Bolte/ ZumaPress/Newscom, 20; Paul Spinelli/AP Images, 22, 27; Mike Segar/Reuters/Newscom, 24–25

Editor: Patrick Donnelly
Series Designer: Sarah Winkler

Publisher's Cataloging-in-Publication Data
Names: Wilner, Barry, author.
Title: Tom Brady vs. Joe Montana / by Barry Wilner.
Other titles: Tom Brady versus Joe Montana
Description: Minneapolis, Minnesota : Abdo Publishing, 2018. | Series: Versus | Includes
     online resources and index.
Identifiers: LCCN 2017946932 | ISBN 9781532113604 (lib.bdg.) | ISBN 9781532152481
     (ebook)
Subjects: LCSH: Football players--United States--Juvenile literature. | Football--Records
     --United States--Juvenile literature. | Sports--History--Juvenile literature.
Classification: DDC 796.332--dc23
LC record available at https://lccn.loc.gov/2017946932

TABLE OF CONTENTS

Introduction...................................04

1 Leadership..................................06

2 Accuracy 12

3 Arm Strength 18

4 Running....................................24

Glossary.....................................30
Online Resources........................31
More Information.........................31
Index...32
About the Author........................32

INTRODUCTION

Playing quarterback in the National Football League (NFL) is one of the most stressful jobs in sports. A good quarterback must be an elite athlete who can withstand crushing hits. He needs to be a quick thinker who can make the right decisions in a split second. He must be a team leader who can execute the coaching staff's game plan. And he has to be comfortable in the spotlight as the face of the team when meeting with fans and the media.

Few have done it better than Joe Montana, whose San Francisco 49ers dominated the 1980s. But Tom Brady of the New England Patriots, the first quarterback to win five Super Bowls, has been amazing as well.

Which one was better? It's an argument without a right or wrong answer. We'll tell their stories and lay out the facts.

BRADY OR MONTANA? YOU DECIDE.

Joe Montana was the picture of cool as he led the 49ers to four Super Bowl victories.

CHAPTER 1

LEADERSHIP

Tom Brady grew up in the region of California known as the Bay Area. It includes San Francisco, Oakland, and the surrounding communities. When Brady was a kid, the San Francisco 49ers were the NFL's top team. They won four Super Bowls between the 1981 and 1989 seasons. Their star quarterback was Joe Montana. Brady idolized him.

"I don't ever see myself like him," Brady said of Montana. "He was so spectacular, and I think he's in a league of his own."

One of the things Brady always wanted to copy was how Montana led his team. When the man known as "Joe Cool" went into the huddle, every 49er knew who was in charge. They followed his lead. If Montana was calm, so were his teammates, no matter how important the game was.

In the Super Bowl after the 1989 season, the 49ers faced the Cincinnati Bengals. That day Montana was at his coolest. The 49ers trailed 16–13 in the final minutes when they got the ball deep in their own territory. As Montana stood in the huddle during a TV timeout, he wasn't looking at the other 49ers. He was calmly looking around, taking in the scenes, when he spotted a familiar face in the crowd.

"Look," he said, "isn't that John Candy?"

It was, indeed, the beloved Canadian actor and comedian. Montana's nervous teammates relaxed when they saw how calm their quarterback was. Then Montana led the 49ers down the field for the game-winning touchdown.

Like his idol, Brady is known for leadership in the tightest times. There's no better example than the Super Bowl after the 2016 season. New England trailed the Atlanta Falcons 28–3 in the third quarter. The Falcons were outplaying the Patriots all over the field. Brady had even thrown an interception that the Falcons returned for a touchdown.

But Brady didn't give up. He told his teammates that if they just went out and played one play at a time, they could still win.

Back they came. Brady threw two touchdown passes in the fourth quarter. He tied the game on a two-point conversion pass to Danny Amendola with 57 seconds left. Then he took the Patriots on a 75-yard drive, which was capped by running back James White's touchdown run to win the first overtime game in Super Bowl history. It was the greatest Super Bowl comeback ever, led by one of the greatest quarterbacks in NFL history.

Another way to show leadership is by how hard you work. It's often said that a team leader should be the first to the locker room each morning and the last to leave every night.

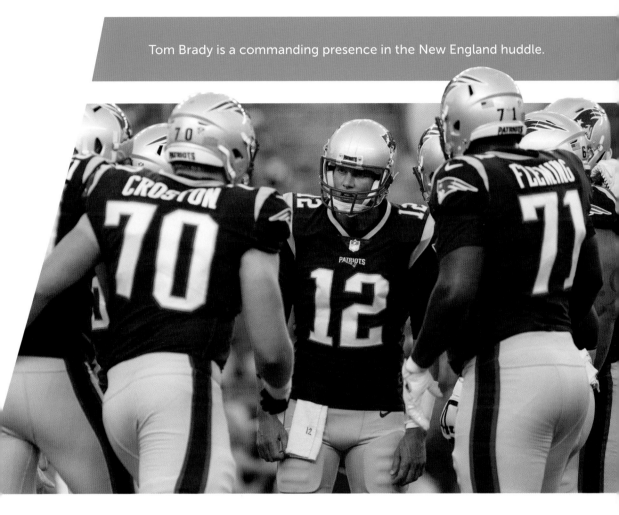

Well, it was almost impossible to beat Montana to the 49ers' clubhouse. And Brady has the same reputation in New England.

Even though both men were among the best ever to play the game, neither ever stopped working to get better. They spent hours and hours watching game film, searching for that one small edge that could lead to victory.

MEET THE PLAYERS

JOE MONTANA

- Born June 11, 1956, in New Eagle, Pennsylvania
- 6 feet, 2 inches/200 pounds
- Attended the University of Notre Dame, 1975–79
- Drafted by the San Francisco 49ers (3rd round/1979)
- Home today: San Francisco, California

TOM BRADY

- Born August 3, 1977, in San Mateo, California
- 6 feet, 4 inches/225 pounds
- Attended the University of Michigan, 1996–2000
- Drafted by the New England Patriots (6th round/2000)
- Home today: Brentwood, California

"Here is a guy that, if he never throws another pass, will be in the Hall of Fame in Canton, Ohio," said Marty Schottenheimer, who coached Montana with the Kansas City Chiefs in Montana's final two NFL seasons. "And yet, he was out there competing and seeking perfection on every pass. It is a sight I will always remember."

Brady played more seasons than Montana, in part because he stayed in such good shape. He's shared his diet and workout plans with other Patriots. They, too, have said they feel stronger and fitter after following Brady's recommendations.

Sometimes, however, leadership shows up even when a player isn't trying to lead. When Montana was hurt late in his career with San Francisco, he was replaced by his talented backup, Steve Young. A few years later, Young won a championship with the 49ers. Much of what he learned from Montana helped Young become a champion.

When Brady missed the first four weeks of the 2016 season, New England's young quarterbacks, Jimmy Garoppolo and Jacoby Brissett, each won games. Again, what they saw Brady do had rubbed off. Brady's ability to lead by example paid big dividends for the Patriots.

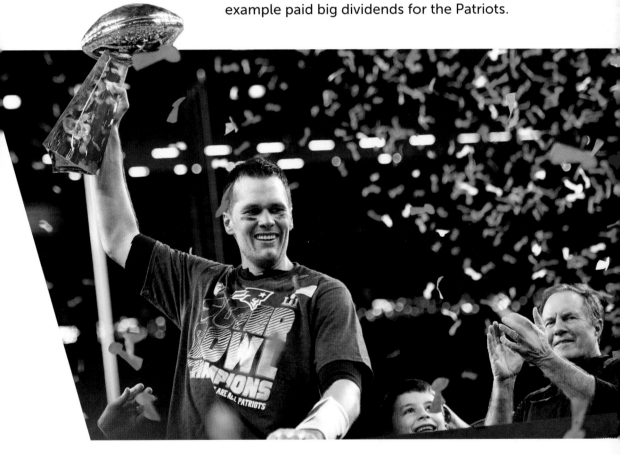

Brady's leadership played a big role in New England's five Super Bowl victories.

Montana's accurate passing helped turn Jerry Rice (80) into a Hall of Fame wide receiver.

CHAPTER 2

ACCURACY

When Bill Walsh became head coach of the San Francisco 49ers in 1979, he immediately began looking for a quarterback. The new guy didn't have to be someone with a cannon for an arm. He didn't have to be a great runner, either.

Walsh wanted someone who was smart, coachable, and maybe most importantly, someone who could put a pass in the perfect place for a receiver. Walsh's preferred offense required an accurate passer, not a hard thrower. He found the right guy.

"One of Joe Montana's most remarkable skills," Walsh said, "was putting the right touch on a pass so that it was easily catchable by a receiver, who often did not have to break stride."

Montana made sure he knew exactly where each of his receivers would be downfield.

Montana was accurate enough to lead the NFL in completion percentage five times. Of course, he had lots of help. San Francisco had top receivers such as Dwight Clark, John Taylor, and Jerry Rice. In fact, Rice is the greatest pass catcher in pro football history. He owes many of his unreachable records to Montana's accuracy.

As amazing as Montana was in the regular season, he was even better in the playoffs and Super Bowls. He completed at least 70 percent of his passes in three of his four Super Bowls. In 1989 when he was the NFL's Most Valuable Player (MVP), he hit on 78.3 percent of his throws. And in his four Super Bowls, Montana went 83 for 122, a 68 percent completion rate. His touchdown-to-interception ratio was 11-to-0.

Rice used to say that his quarterback could close his eyes and still put the ball exactly where it needed to be. But there was no magic to Montana's skills. His accuracy was built on more concrete traits. First, he knew where everyone on his team should be on every play. He usually knew how the defense would line up, too, as well as where the weak spots were in that defense.

Montana also understood it was never about how hard he threw the ball, but where he threw it. Quarterbacks sometimes have to search for air lanes between defenders to get their passes through to their receivers. Montana rarely had to search—he knew where those lanes would be.

One more thing: Montana never was bothered by weather. He grew up in western Pennsylvania and went to college at Notre Dame in northwestern Indiana. Cold, wind, and snow couldn't slow him.

Brady has that same ability, even though he grew up in California. Brady went to college in Michigan, where he learned that good quarterbacks must adapt to all conditions. Wet ball, frozen field, howling winds? So what?

Montana was 82nd pick of the 1979 NFL Draft. Getting a Hall of Fame quarterback in the third round of the draft was quite a steal for the 49ers. But the Patriots were even more fortunate. Brady was the 199th pick in 2000. It might be the best draft choice in NFL history.

PROFESSIONAL SUCCESS

JOE MONTANA

- NFL debut: September 16, 1979
- Years active: 1979–94
- Super Bowl record: 4 appearances, 4 victories
- First team All-Pro: 1987, 1989, 1990

TOM BRADY

- NFL debut: November 23, 2000
- Years active: 2000–present
- Super Bowl record: 7 appearances, 5 victories
- First team All-Pro: 2007, 2010

Brady didn't start any games in his rookie year. When he took over for injured starter Drew Bledsoe in the second game of the 2001 season, the Patriots offense was focused on the running game. Very soon that changed. Patriots coaches saw how accurate Brady was—something that was as true in his 17th pro season as it was in his first. Given more freedom to pass through the years, Brady got better and better.

One of his great skills is what quarterbacks call "throwing receivers open." That means Brady can throw the ball to a spot while his target is covered. He knows the receiver and only the receiver will get in position to make the catch.

Brady has played with different receivers almost yearly. Some of his targets have been outstanding receivers, such as Randy Moss, Rob Gronkowski, Wes Welker, and Julian Edelman. But he often needs to learn the habits of multiple new receivers each summer. Yet Brady still turns most of those receivers into effective weapons, and New England keeps winning.

One of the only ways to shake up Brady is to put pressure on him. A strong pass rush can force him to throw too soon or while he's off balance. Atlanta did a good job of that in the 2016 Super Bowl—for three and a half quarters. Then Brady led a comeback for the ages with his crisp, accurate passing.

"You've got to affect Tom Brady somehow," Falcons linebacker Vic Beasley said. "You've got to hit him and get him off the spot somehow, because if you don't touch him, it's going to be a long day for you, because he's just a flawless quarterback."

Brady leads Rob Gronkowski with a pass in 2015.

Brady's arm has to be strong enough to pass the ball in the blustery New England winter weather.

CHAPTER 3

ARM STRENGTH

Brett Favre could throw a football almost the length of the field. So can Joe Flacco and Cam Newton. Montana and Brady? Not in their dreams. When it was time to uncork a deep throw to a streaking wide receiver, Montana and Brady could do it. But the long ball wasn't their primary strength.

It helps a quarterback to have a strong arm. But Montana and Brady both would admit that throwing 60-yard passes was not their top skill. In fact, NFL.com once ranked Brady outside the top 10 in the league in arm strength. Had a similar study been conducted during Montana's career, it surely would have listed him pretty far down, too.

One reason Brady lasted until the 199th pick of the 2000 draft was his suspect arm strength. Yet through his record-setting time in the NFL, Brady has gotten better at the power game. He hasn't improved to the level of current bombers Matthew Stafford or Ben Roethlisberger. But neither of them has won five Super Bowls. Nor has any other quarterback.

Brady doesn't often throw the long ball, but he's got enough arm strength to be successful when he airs it out.

IN THE SPOTLIGHT

JOE MONTANA

- Super Bowl stats: 83 for 122, 1,142 yards, 11 touchdowns, 0 interceptions in 4 games
- Career highlight: Hooked up with Dwight Clark for "The Catch" to beat the Dallas Cowboys and put the 49ers in the Super Bowl for the first time in January 1982.
- Awards: Super Bowl MVP (after the 1981, 1984, and 1989 seasons), NFL MVP (1989, 1990)
- Playoff record: 16–7

TOM BRADY

- Super Bowl stats: 207 for 309, 2,071 yards, 15 touchdowns, 5 interceptions in 7 games
- Career highlight: Brought the Patriots back from a 28–3 deficit to defeat the Atlanta Falcons for the biggest comeback win in Super Bowl history in February 2017.
- Awards: Super Bowl MVP (after the 2001, 2003, 2014, and 2016 seasons), NFL MVP (2007, 2010)
- Playoff record: 25–9

Brady credits his workouts and his diet for the improvement in how far he can throw a football. "Your body for an athlete is what your asset is," Brady said. "If your body breaks down and you can't perform, then you have no job. I've tried to learn the right ways to take care of your body."

Montana, meanwhile, rarely needed to throw the ball a long way. The West Coast Offense, which he ran in San Francisco and brought with him to Kansas City, was built on short passes

Not blessed with a huge arm, Montana could still step into a throw and get some zip on the ball.

and perfect timing. No team in NFL history was better at piling up yards after the catch than Montana's 49ers, because his accuracy allowed his receivers to catch the ball in stride.

Sure, Montana put plenty of strength behind his short throws, getting them exactly where they needed to be. But most of his touchdown throws came from near the end zone or on quick passes that Rice and company turned into long gains.

Why is arm strength important for a quarterback? One reason is weather. The more power on a throw, the more likely it will go where it's aimed, even in windy or wet conditions.

Another reason is the strengths of a receiving corps. If a quarterback has a great deep threat at receiver—Brady had Moss for a few years; Montana had Rice—the best way to take advantage of that can be with the long ball.

There's also the fear factor for defenders. A cornerback or safety is less likely to gamble against a passer with a great arm. He knows there's a good chance he could give up a long completion if he lets the receiver get behind him.

Besides, having a big arm sometimes gets a quarterback in trouble. For instance, Favre seemed to think he could throw the ball through defenders. When he retired, Favre held most major passing records—including most interceptions.

The fact that neither Montana nor Brady was close to the top in arm strength was actually never a problem for them. They simply did everything else so well that they became superstars.

Another Super Bowl–winning quarterback, Brad Johnson of the 2002 Tampa Bay Buccaneers, points out that not having a rifle for an arm isn't so bad. "Arm strength is the most overrated part of football," Johnson said. "The most important thing about a quarterback is knowing the system, understanding where everyone is, quickness with your feet, accuracy, and throwing a ball that's catchable. It's not throwing a ball real hard. Very rarely do you see a ball thrown over 40 yards."

Brady rushes for a 6-yard touchdown against the Oakland Raiders in a January 2002 playoff game.

CHAPTER 4

RUNNING

Michael Vick, Cam Newton, and Russell Wilson have proven to be among the most dynamic quarterbacks the NFL has ever seen. No one knew when they might take off on a scramble. Defenses always had to be ready for those quarterbacks to run.

Brady will laugh when asked about his running skills. He has said he doesn't think he's the fastest person in his family, let alone on the New England Patriots roster.

Montana was a bit better when forced to take off with the ball. When he was at Notre Dame, NFL scouts liked his versatility. He could pass from a straight dropback. He could pass on the move. And he could run.

But throwing was always his strength, just as it was for Brady. Not that either has been afraid to run, especially when he was about to be sacked.

In his 14-season career with the 49ers and Chiefs, Montana gained

Montana used his quickness to avoid pass rushers and keep the play alive long enough for a receiver to get open.

457 rushing yards. He scored 20 touchdowns. His longest run was 21 yards.

As for Brady, during his first 17 seasons in New England, he rushed for 940 yards and 17 touchdowns. His longest run was 22 yards.

Brady, though, is a master of the quarterback sneak. He'll lean low behind a blocker and surge ahead for first downs and touchdowns.

Montana once said that scrambling turned a quarterback into a sixth possible runner or receiver. Defenses usually only were ready for five. They assumed the quarterback would just be passing. Advantage: Montana.

He also explained that a good quarterback knew when and where to run. Most importantly he also knew when to get out of bounds or slide before being tackled.

Maybe Montana didn't have the grace of Rice; the power of Tom Rathman, the 49ers' strong fullback; or the speed of

Montana's running ability gave the 49ers offense an added dimension.

Ricky Watters, one of San Francisco's top running backs. But Montana could do just enough to keep defenses off balance with the threat of a scramble.

"Montana is such a great athlete," Hall of Fame coach Don Shula of the Miami Dolphins once said. "He's a pocket passer, he comes out by design on the rollout and the bootleg, and he makes plays on the scramble. He'll wiggle around and come up with the big play."

Montana did that time and again in the Super Bowl after the 1984 season. He was the MVP of that 38–16 win over Shula's Dolphins, in part because of his work on the ground. Montana ran the ball five times for 59 yards on the day, and when he scampered into the end zone from 6 yards out in the second quarter, the Niners took a 21–10 lead and didn't look back.

Brady, of course, won his fifth Super Bowl in February 2017 and was still going strong at age 40. Even at that advanced age, Brady could take off for a big gain on the ground at a key time. For example, in his first game of 2017, Brady scrambled for a first down. He was tackled out of bounds, got up, and celebrated by posing like Olympic sprinter Usain Bolt.

That was a bit of an exaggeration on his part—Brady doesn't really have sprinter's speed. But he's quick enough to make defenders miss, and when they don't, he's big enough to make them pay. Against Miami in 2014, Brady rumbled for a 17-yard gain. As Dolphins safety Walt Aikens got ready to tackle him, Brady lowered his shoulder and delivered his own hit.

It was the kind of play a team leader is expected to make. Brady and Montana made their careers on plays just like it.

LEGACY

JOE MONTANA

- Important records: Tied for most Super Bowl victories without a loss (4); tied for most seasons leading modern NFL in completion percentage (5)
- Key rivals: Ken Anderson, Dan Marino, Jim Kelly
- Off-field accomplishments: Established the Four Rings Montana Family Foundation to help underprivileged children in the San Francisco Bay Area; also supports Feeding America, Multiple Myeloma Research Foundation, and the Muhammad Ali Parkinson Center

"There's no thrill like throwing a touchdown pass."

— Joe Montana

TOM BRADY

- Important records: Most Super Bowl victories by a quarterback (5); first to win four Super Bowl MVP Awards
- Key rivals: Peyton Manning, Eli Manning, Ben Roethlisberger
- Off-field accomplishments: Supports Best Buddies International and the Boys & Girls Clubs of America

"When you're one of the leaders of the team, there are no days off."

— Tom Brady

GLOSSARY

COMPLETION PERCENTAGE
A statistic that measures how often a quarterback's passes are caught by his receivers.

CORNERBACK
A defensive player who normally covers wide receivers.

DRAFT
A system that allows teams to acquire new players coming into a league.

END ZONE
The end of the field where teams try to score touchdowns.

HUDDLE
Where players on offense and defense each meet on the field to call plays.

INTERCEPTION
A pass intended for an offensive player that is caught by a defensive player.

SACK
A tackle of the quarterback behind the line of scrimmage before he can pass the ball.

SCOUT
A person whose job is to look for talented young players.

SCRAMBLE
To run around with the ball behind the line of scrimmage while looking for an open receiver.

VERSATILITY
Ability to do many things.

Online Resources

Booklinks
NONFICTION NETWORK
FREE! ONLINE NONFICTION RESOURCES

To learn more about great quarterbacks, visit abdobooklinks.com. These links are routinely monitored and updated to provide the most current information available.

More Information

Books

Gitlin, Marty. *Tom Brady: Super Bowl Quarterback*. Minneapolis, MN: Abdo Publishing, 2012.

Myers, Dan. *Make Me the Best Football Player*. Minneapolis, MN: Abdo Publishing, 2017.

Wilner, Barry. *The Super Bowl*. Minneapolis, MN: Abdo Publishing, 2013.

INDEX

Aikens, Walt, 28

Amendola, Danny, 8

Bledsoe, Drew, 16

Bolt, Usain, 28

Brissett, Jacoby, 11

Candy, John, 8

Clark, Dwight, 14, 21

Edelman, Julian, 16

Favre, Brett, 19, 23

Flacco, Joe, 19

Garoppolo, Jimmy, 11

Gronkowski, Rob, 16

Moss, Randy, 16, 23

Newton, Cam, 19, 25

Rathman, Tom, 27

Rice, Jerry, 14, 15, 22, 23, 27

Roethlisberger, Ben, 20, 29

Schottenheimer, Marty, 10

Stafford, Matthew, 20

Super Bowl, 4, 7–8, 14–15, 16, 17, 20, 21, 23, 28, 29

Taylor, John, 14

University of Michigan, 10, 15

University of Notre Dame, 10, 15, 25

Vick, Michael, 25

Walsh, Bill, 13

Watters, Ricky, 27–28

Welker, Wes, 16

White, James, 8

Wilson, Russell, 25

Young, Steve, 11

ABOUT THE AUTHOR

Barry Wilner has been a sports writer for the Associated Press since 1976. He has covered every Super Bowl since 1987. Barry also has written more than 60 books and is an adjunct professor at Manhattanville College in New York. He lives in Garnerville, New York.